Tales In Verse
— FROM —
Distant Lands

STORIES FOR CHILDREN TOLD IN VERSE

SRIVIDYA BALAKRISHNAN

INDIA · SINGAPORE · MALAYSIA

Notion Press

No. 8, 3rd Cross Street,
CIT Colony, Mylapore,
Chennai, Tamil Nadu - 600 004

First Published by Notion Press 2020
Copyright © Srividya Balakrishnan 2020
All Rights Reserved.

ISBN 978-1-64850-639-0

This book has been published with all efforts taken to make the material error-free after the consent of the author. However, the author and the publisher do not assume and hereby disclaim any liability to any party for any loss, damage, or disruption caused by errors or omissions, whether such errors or omissions result from negligence, accident, or any other cause.

While every effort has been made to avoid any mistake or omission, this publication is being sold on the condition and understanding that neither the author nor the publishers or printers would be liable in any manner to any person by reason of any mistake or omission in this publication or for any action taken or omitted to be taken or advice rendered or accepted on the basis of this work. For any defect in printing or binding the publishers will be liable only to replace the defective copy by another copy of this work then available.

Dedication

This book is dedicated to **Shalu**, a dear friend.

Contents

Preface 7

Chapter 1.	The Singer and the Dolphin. 9
Chapter 2.	The Summer of St. Martin. 13
Chapter 3.	Metabo and Camille. 17
Chapter 4.	The Mystery of the Sphinx. 21
Chapter 5.	The Two Bears in the Sky. 25
Chapter 6.	The Flowers from the Moon. 29
Chapter 7.	Hanaca's Hat 33
Chapter 8.	How Deserts Were Formed. 37
Chapter 9.	The Three Sheikhs and the Queen of Arabia. 41
Chapter 10.	King Solomon, The Wise. 45
Chapter 11.	King Solomon's Vase. 49
Chapter 12.	Why the Sun and the Moon Live in the Sky. 53
Chapter 13.	Manu's Justice 57
Chapter 14.	Lord Ganesha and the Fruit of Paradise. . 61

Contents

Chapter 15.	King Pari and the Creeper	65
Chapter 16.	The Tsar and the Mugik (A Russian Peasant)	69
Chapter 17.	The Lute-Playing Queen	73
Chapter 18.	Vassilia the Beautiful Weaver	77
Chapter 19.	Father Christmas's Workshop	81
Chapter 20.	The Christmas Lunch	85

Preface

Tales in verse from distant lands is a collection of poems, each poem telling a legend or a fable in simple verse for young readers though many of the stories have universal appeal. Parents and teachers will find that this opens a window to the world and encourages extended reading.

"The singer and the dolphin," a Greek legend, for instance, tells the story of a famous singer who uses his talent to escape from thieves and attackers.

"The Summer of St Martin" tells of the goodness of Martin which makes even God bend the rules.

"Metabo and Camille" is the story of an ingenious javelin thrower who saves himself and his daughter through his out-of-the-box thinking.

"The mystery of the sphinx" shows the wit of the famous Oedipus.

"Two bears in the sky" is a fantastical take on the origin of constellations.

"Hanaca's hat" is the sweet story of a lovely girl ridiculed by all till a secret is revealed which changes her life story.

Preface

The tales of King Solomon and the Queen of Arabia make for interesting reading with morals thrown in for good measure. The Indian stories of Manu, Pari and Lord Ganesha are popular folklore known to many, enjoyable in verse. The Russian story of Vassilia tells of how a bright young girl's talent makes her queen. Finally, Father Christmas and the Christmas lunch bring alive the celebrations of the holiday season.

These stories have been taken from various adaptations of folklore and legends from across the world.

The Singer and the Dolphin
(Greek Legend)

*Can a person save his life
through his singing? Find out*

In ancient world
Lived Arion
Of the most famous singers
He was one.

In Sicily
In a festival once
As prize golden cups
And jewels he won.

To take all these
To Corinth his home,
He hired a ship
And was homeward bound.

But the sailors were jealous
Of his prizes galore,
So they attacked the singer
To throw him overboard.

Arion requested
For one last song
Which he wanted to sing,
Before he was gone.

The sailors granted
His last wish.
To listen to his song
Was pure bliss.

So enchanted were the sailors
By his song,
They were hardly aware
Of what was going on.

His first few notes,
So melodious were they
A dolphin was attracted
As it swam along the way.

It came to the side
Of Arion's ship
And swam along listening
To his music.

He jumped overboard
On to its back.
And was thus saved,
From the sailors' attack.

He was carried back
Across the sea,
Home to Corinth
As fast as could be.

When the ship reached Corinth
The sailors lied
That in a storm in the sea,
The singer had died.

Much to their amazement
Arion showed up
With a band of soldiers
And their game was up.

There was erected
By the people then
A statue in memory
Of this event.

A young man on the back
Of a dolphin.
The statue is still there
In the port of Corinth.

The Singer on the Dolphin

The Summer of St. Martin
(Italian Legend)

*This is the legend behind warm days
in the cold month of November.
Even God bends rules when Man is very good*

On a November day
Long ago,
It was raining hard
The heavens poured.

A young soldier
Martin by name
Rode on a horse
On a country lane.

On the way,
He saw a man
Dressed in rags
Cold and wan.

Martin stopped
So filled was he

With human love
And sympathy.

He took out a sword
And sliced in two
His heavy cloak
That was brand new.

He gave one half
To the man so poor.
A kindly act
It was for sure.

But on the way
And in the gale
Was another man
Naked and pale.

From rain and storm
The man to save
The another half
Of his cloak he gave.

Now Martin too
Was cold and wet.
To give to others
Nothing was left.

But he still felt pity
For the poor folk

Who were cold and wet
And had no clothes.

All of a sudden God
Stopped the rain,
Banished the clouds
It was warm again.

High in the sky
The sun shone bright,
Spreading around
Its warm light.

God changed the weather
By his goodness impressed.
Martin as saint
The heavens blessed.

Ever since then
When the sun shines,
In the first fortnight
In November time,
And there are
A few warm days,
Everyone who knows
This story says,
The summer of St Martin is this,
Nature's way of giving him a kiss.

A warm day in November

Metabo and Camille
(Roman Legend)

Read on and see how the intelligence of a javelin thrower saved lives

Once upon a time,
A long time ago
Lived in Rome
King Metabo.

A famous javelin thrower
Was he,
Better than him
No man could be.

Once with his daughter
Named Camille,
He set off hunting
In the jungle.

Suddenly as if
From nowhere,
His enemies attacked him,
Then and there.

With his young daughter
He fled from the same,
Till to a fast flowing
River he came.

Across the river he was
Unable to swim,
With his daughter on his back,
Clinging to him.

It seemed he was lost
Until he thought,
Of an intelligent and
Bold way out.

His daughter,
To his javelin he tied,
And with all his strength threw it
To the river's other side.

Then he dived into the river
And swam across
To the place
Where Camille was.

His enemies were
So amazed,
They gave up the chase
And left the place.

Metabo throws his daughter tied to a javelin across the river

The Mystery of the Sphinx
(Greek Legend)

How intelligent was Oedipus?
Well, he was the only one who
could solve the riddle of the sphinx

The city of Thebes in olden days,
Was guarded by the Sphinx, they say.
A lion's body it possessed
With eagle's wings and woman's head.
It asked a riddle much the same
Of every passerby who came.
And when they could not answer it,
It consumed them bit by bit.
When Oedipus came there one day,
The Sphinx refused to give way,
Unless he answered with some wit
To the question put by it.
Asked the Sphinx "What being,
Has four legs in the morning,
Two in the middle of the day
In the evening three, say if you may?"

"Man" said Oedipus and smiled,
"He crawls on all fours as a child,
Walks on two legs when young and bold
And leans on a stick when he is old."

The Sphinx

The Two Bears in the Sky
(The Brothers Grimm)

*Have you heard of the two constellations
'The Big Dipper and the Little Dipper' or
'The Great Bear and the Little Bear'?
This is the story that connects 2 real bears
with the two constellations.*

Hans the young giant,
Was helpful and kind
And a stronger person than him,
Was hard to find.

By two bears his village
Was once attacked,
One male, one female
Back to back.

Scattered the townsfolk
In great fear,
To whom in this world
Is life not dear?

The Two Bears in the Sky

The mayor and the people
Of the town
Rushed to find Hans
Before sundown.

"Help us, Hans,"
The townsfolk said
"For the two bears are dancing
On our heads."

To find the bears
Hans was game.
He found them scaring
A poor old dame.

Leapt Hans on the larger
Without a sound,
Seized it by the arm
And swung it around.

Round and round
And ever so high
He flung the bear
Into the sky.

Then he did the same
To its mate
But the female was smaller
With a different fate.

The Two Bears in the Sky

She flew higher in the sky
Than the male
Who watched her go by
So goes the tale.

"Come over here."
He called out loud
"I can't" she replied
"I don't know how."

"You come over here."
She shouted back
But the bear couldn't
For strength he lacked.

So the two roam around
One after the other
Trying to get back
Again together.

"Great Bear and Little Bear"
By watchers of the sky,
They are called now
And you know why.

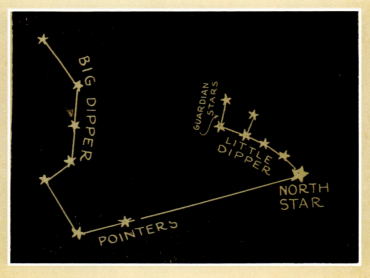

The constellations, the Great bear and the
Little Bear

The Flowers from the Moon
(Alpine legend)

*How did alpine flowers come to the Earth?
Read on and find out*

High up in the mountains
Lived a prince
A gentler, nicer person
Has never lived since.

To the moon once
He wished to go ,
Because he loved
Its gentle glow.

His dream came true
One beautiful night
So he found out the source
Of the cool moonlight.

Which came from the Moonking's
Beautiful daughter,
With a lovely face
And a tinkling laughter.

The two found a place
In each other's hearts.
But the Moonking said sadly
You both have to part.

To different worlds
Do you belong,
To bear the separation
You must be strong.

As a sign of her love
The moonking's daughter
Gave to the prince
One of moon's flowers.

Which were smooth and lovely,
Covered the moon like snow,
So the first alpine flower
Was brought to earth you know.

Alpine flowers

Hanaca's Hat
(Japanese Tale)

Who was Hanaca? Why did she wear a hat?
The wind blew it away.
What happened after that?

There was a girl called Hanaca,
Who always wore a hat.
How long she had worn it
No one knew about that.

Her father before he died
Put it on her head
And she could never take it off
Since then, it was said.

Everyone made fun of her
And it hurt her so,
That she decided to leave the town
And in the king's service go.

But even there the servants,
True to her fears,

Would laugh at her hat
And leave her in tears.

One day, the king's son,
A very comely lad
Came upon Hanaca
Looking really sad.

On listening to her story
So sorry was he,
He wanted to marry her
As soon as could be.

But when the king came
To know of their affair,
He banished Hanaca
From his palace then and there.

Tearfully she turned
Toward the palace gates,
When a great gust of wind
Her wide brimmed hat displaced.

With the hat gone
Now the people could see,
That Hanaca was indeed
An extraordinary beauty.

The precious jewels on her hair
Had the people surprised.
As a daughter of a samurai,
She was recognized.

So the king allowed
The marriage after all.
In honour of the couple
There was a great ball.

And the people were happy
And everyone was gay
And this story is remembered
Till this day.

Hanaca wearing hat

How Deserts Were Formed
(Arabian Tale)

First God made Earth full of Gardens. Then what happened? How did the deserts arise?

On the day of creation,
In the beginning of time,
The Lord made the world
The earth was at its prime.

The Lord made it with
His varied powers.
It was one huge
Garden of flowers.

Then He called Man
And this warning gave
The beauty of this world
Depends on how you behave.

Every time you do
A wrong thing, my man
On the earth will fall
A grain of sand.

No attention was paid
To this warning by man,
For what harm could be done
By a few grains of sand?

He continued to do,
All kinds of wicked things,
Forgetting that every act,
Its own reaction brings.

Then little by little,
The few grains of sand
Grew into seas and rivers
And invaded the land.

The great wide deserts
Were formed thus
What man gets is
According to what he does.

Gardens turn into deserts

The Three Sheikhs and the Queen of Arabia
(Arabian Tale)

How did the queen choose her king amongst the many suitors?

There was a Queen of Arabia,
Maura was her name.
So beautiful and powerful was she
Far and wide was her fame.

Many suitors came,
To her husband be,
One by one she discarded
Till the list was reduced to three.

All the three suitors
Were rich and young and fair,
Among them her partner,
She had to choose with care.

One night she disguised herself
And went into their tents.

And something to eat for dinner,
She asked of each of them.

The first, a real miser,
Gave her left over food,
The second tasteless camel's tail,
Which was hardly good.

The third sheikh was courteous,
Hakim was his name,
He gave her tender meat to eat.
And himself shared the same.

Her rich suitors the next day
The queen called to the court,
And offered them the same meals,
They had given the night before.

Hakim got fresh and tasty food
But he refused to eat
Till he could share with the others
The rich and succulent meat.

Queen Maura told her suitors,
The most generous of you three
Is Sheikh Hakim and so
He will my husband be.

The queen feeding her suitors

King Solomon, The Wise
(Arabian Fable)

How did Solomon become so wise?

King Solomon
On a hunt one day
Saw two snakes
Fighting away.

The larger was white
The smaller black
But poisonous fangs,
The smaller had.

Just as the black one
Was about to bite,
King Solomon
Intervened in the fight.

And killed it with a stone,
Aimed from high,
And saved the white snake
Which was going to die.

Safe at last it went,
Off in the woods,
Far away from
Where Solomon stood.

Sometime later
Solomon met
A giant in the woods
A cause to fret?

But the giant said,
"Be not afraid
I am the white snake
You bravely saved."

"The black snake
Was my poisonous foe
Ask for a gift
As my thanks, you know."

"You can have one"
Solomon was told,
"A gift of healing
Or a gift of gold."

"Neither" said Solomon
With a smile,
"A gift of wisdom"
Would be worth my while."

"You shall have it"
The giant said,
"In abundance."
And nodded his head.

This is how
As the story is told,
Solomon became the wisest
In the world.

King Solomon in his court

King Solomon's Vase
(Arabian Fable)

Solomon's mastery over his subjects is tested in this story of the vase

King Solomon was
So wise and just
God gave him mastery over
All his subjects.

Spirits and demons were
Under his command,
So too were the animals
Of his land.

Queen Sheeba wanted
To put him to test,
If indeed he was
The very best.

She sent him an envoy
With a vase,
Who said to the king
"Best wishes, Your grace."

'Can you with all
Your powers guess,
What is the present
I bring your highness?"

A spirit whispered in
Solomon's ear,
"A pearl and an emerald
Are in there."

The king the envoy
This answer told,
Who answered "Very well,
But please behold,"

"There is a tiny hole,
In each stone,
Pass a thread through them.
Can this be done?"

A demon told the king
The best jeweller's name
But even he could not
Do the same.

Then a tiny voice
Came from the ground,
"May I help Your Majesty?"
Said the source of the sound.

The entire court looked
In great surprise,
It was a worm that said this,
To Solomon, the wise.

In no time,
Accomplished the worm,
The task the best jeweller,
Could not perform.

When she heard the story
The Queen realised,
That Solomon was indeed
Just and wise.

It was true that
No ruler could stand
Against a king
Who could command
Not only spirits
And demons too,
But even the worms
His work to do.

The vase in Solomon's court

Why the Sun and the Moon Live in the Sky
(African Fable)

Why indeed?

Eons ago
In the beginning of time,
Lived the Sun and the Moon
In their prime.

A married couple
Were the two,
And lived on earth
Which was then brand new.

Great friends they were
Of the beautiful sea
Who lived nearby,
As blue as could be.

They invited the sea
For a visit one day.

But the sea hesitated
And this message relayed.

"I am big and vast"
Said the deep blue sea,
"Is there room in your house,
To accommodate me?"

The Sun and the Moon
Reassured the sea,
And invited her to dinner
With her whole family.

This you will see
Was the biggest mistake
The Sun and the Moon
Were ever to make.

Along came the sea
With animals galore,
The fish and the crabs
And snakes and more.

Immediately, the water
Began to rise.
The Sun and the Moon
Were really surprised.

To avoid being drowned
They climbed to the roof.
That the visit was a mistake
This was proof.

Then they climbed up
Into the sky.
There they remain now
And you know why.

The sun, the moon and the sea

Manu's Justice
(Indian Fable)

Even the son of the king is not above the law

There was once a Chola king
Far and wide was his fame.
Renowned was he for his justice
Manu was his name.

He had hung a bell on the palace gate,
For his subjects to ring,
Whenever they had a problem
To set before the king.

The King's only son once set out
For a ride one day,
In the palace Chariot,
But a calf came in the way.

The young prince to stop his steed
Valiantly tried,
But alas, the wayward calf
Instantly died.

Manu's Justice

The calf's mother, the holy cow
Came running to the place,
She could not save her only calf
Being seconds late.

With tears streaming down her eyes,
The palace bell she rang.
When Manu found the story out
His heart felt a pang.

For in the court of justice
Stood his only son,
But the law of his land
Was same for everyone.

On his chariot, steeling his heart,
He rode over his son.
An eye for an eye, a tooth for tooth,
Justice for the cow was done.

With the king's just ruling,
Even the Gods were pleased.
They brought to life both calf and son,
And the king from his pain released.

A fairer and more just king
Never was, they say,
And stories of his justice
Are remembered till this day.

A scene from Manu's story depicted outside Madras High court, India

Lord Ganesha and the Fruit of Paradise
(Indian Mythological Story)

My parents are my world.
How did Ganesha prove it?

On Mount Kailas sat Lord Shiva
With consort Parvathy,
And their servants and two sons,
In happy camaraderie.

The Elephant God was the elder,
Lord Ganesha was his name.
Lord Karthik was the younger
And they were playing games.

Along came Naradmuni,
A sage both old and wise.
He offered to Lord Shiva
The Fruit of Paradise.

"But," he said "This Fruit,
Only one person should eat,

For then he would be strong and wise,
And many benefits reap."

Now Lord Shiva as they say
Was caught in a real fix
For sons he had two and fruit one
Now which son should he pick?

So he told his sons, the Fruit,
Will go to him who goes,
Around the world in the shortest time,
Who speed and smartness knows.

Lord Karthik on his peacock,
Set off across the globe,
Leaving behind the Elephant God
On his mouse to carry his load.

But Lord Ganesha—the Elephant God,
Though fat was very smart.
He went around his Parents
With folded hands and heart.

"For you are my world, my parents,
My life to you belongs.
With you by my side to guide
I can never go wrong."

When Lord Karthik come back later,
Lord Shiva smiled and said,
"The Elephant God deserved the Fruit
For he used both heart and head."

"Parents bring us into this world,
And lead us by the hand.
They are our guide in difficult times,
This we should understand.
They are our world, the reason,
That we are here today,
This we should remember
And love them always."

Lord Ganesha with the Fruit Of Paradise

King Pari and the Creeper
(Indian Fable)

Can even the creeper be helped?

King Pari was a gentleman,
And a very generous king.
People across his happy land
Did his praises sing.

On his chariot once,
He went out for a ride.
He saw a creeper growing
Along the roadside.

Now, as you know a creeper,
Is a plant that grows,
Along the ground or on the wall
Or around a support.

But the plant the king saw,
Was lying on the ground.
There was no support
For it to grow around.

King Pari stopped his chariot,
And thought and thought awhile.
Then he got down by the roadside
Bent down with a smile.

He picked up the creeper
And wrapped it around
His palace chariot
Without a sound.

His chariot provided
The creeper support,
Big and strong
For it to grow.

Back home to his palace
He set off on foot.
Leaving his chariot
Behind for good.

His generosity,
People say,
Was hailed by all,
Since that day.

The creeper supported by the chariot

The Tsar and the Mugik (A Russian Peasant)
(A Russian Tale)

The story of a Russian peasant who presented a riddle to the Tsar.

A Russian Tsar was passing,
By a field one day,
When he saw a mugik working
Hard and sweating away.

He stopped and watched the mugik,
His subjects' lot to learn,
He asked the Russian peasant
"How much do you earn?"

"Eighty roubles, Sire."
The Russian peasant said
"And how do you spend it?"
Asked the country's head

"A quarter goes in taxes,
A quarter pays my debts,

The Tsar and the Mugik (A Russian Peasant)

I lend another quarter,
And throw out what is left."

The Russian peasant's answer
Was confusing to his guest
Who said "I got the taxes,
But please explain the rest."

"I keep, maintain my father,
And thus I pay the debt,
For having brought me up,"
The mugik smiled and said,

"I loan my son money,
To study and then earn,
He will then support me,
When I am old and infirm."

"The money for my daughter's
Maintenance I pay,
Is lost to me, she will marry,
And leave me one day."

So pleased was the Tsar
By the peasant's wit,
He used this as a riddle
To wager courtiers with.

The money that was so won
By the Tsar was sent,
To the Russian mugik
With best compliments.

The Tsar wagers the riddle in his court

The Lute-Playing Queen
(Russian Tale)

Story about how the lute saved the king

The Crusades were on,
People made war.
The Turks took prisoner
Russia's Tsar.

He wrote at once
Back home to his wife,
To pay his ransom,
And free him for life.

But no message came
From his hometown
The Tsar could only wait
Feeling let down.

Sometime later
After some days,
Came a Lute-playing lad
To the Sultan's palace.

At his musical strain,
So good was he,
That the Turk Lord
Was pleased as could be.

Anything in his kingdom,
He told him to take,
For his wonderful songs
Payment to make.

The Lute player asked
The Tsar as his slave,
The Sultan agreed
The Tsar he gave.

The two journeyed
A long, long way,
Till the capitol of Russia,
They reached one day.

The lute player set there
Free his slave,
Bade farewell and went,
No reason he gave.

The return of the Tsar,
Caused great joy.
It brought a smile
To every girl and boy.

But the Tsar felt let down,
Angered in life,
Refused completely
To see his wife.

Planned he to put her
To death, alas,
Uncaring queen
He thought she was.

Then he heard,
The gentle strains of a lute.
They were those of his saviour
He could not dispute.

The mysterious musician
He stared in surprise,
Was his wife, the Tsarina,
In disguise.

At the reunion
The city rejoiced
Their thanks for the queen
The subjects voiced.

Queen playing the lute

Vassilia the Beautiful Weaver
(Russian Tale)

Talent takes you places — literally

There was once an orphan,
In the land of Russia,
A beautiful young weaver,
Named Vassilia.

She was taken in,
By a good old dame,
And wished to thank her,
For the same.

So she took some flax,
And used her time,
To make a thread,
That was ever so fine.

She wove it on
A special frame,
From which a very fine
And soft cloth came.

She gave the cloth
To the woman to sell,
To repay her for
Looking after her well.

"What a beautiful cloth"
The old dame said,
"Only one is worthy of this,
The country's head."

So she took it to court,
Gave it to the Tsar
Who said , "I will pay,
Whatever you ask."
But the old woman said,
"I brought it as a gift."
The Tsar was very pleased
To receive it.

But to cut the fine cloth,
And a shirt to make,
No tailor would,
The responsibility take.

The old woman then
Told his Highness,
Vassilia would
Make the shirt best.

Then the young maid
To work set,
To make a shirt
That was just perfect.

Then she herself
Took it to court.
When the Tsar saw her,
He was floored.

So impressed was he
By her beauty,
He asked her to marry him,
As soon as could be.

So they married and lived
For a long, long time,
In happiness and
Domestic bliss sublime.

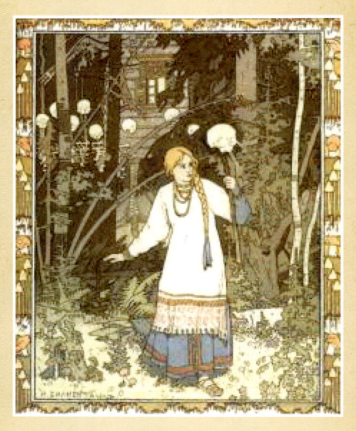

The beautiful Vassilia

Father Christmas's Workshop
(American Folklore)

Do you know how hard Santa Claus works throughout the year to get you your presents on time?

At his workshop
In the North Pole,
Works Father Christmas
Through the year whole.

What does he work on,
Do you ask?
He is engaged
In an important task.

He has to make
The toys you see,
For children
At Christmas time to receive.

A tough job it is,
Needs imagination

And also skill
and organization.

In this massive work
Helped is he,
By the gnomes of the North
Who are as fast as could be.

Though sometimes
They do mischief,
Most of the time
They listen to their chief.

Once all is done,
He loads up his sled,
Harnesses the reindeer
Strong and well-fed.

With his merriest laugh
On a face that is bright,
With a crack of his whip
Which resounds in the night,

He flies out
Of the North Pole,
Our Father Christmas
Who's grand and old.

All over the world then
Father Christmas goes,
The night before Christmas
Everybody knows.

To all the little children
Be it girl or boy,
He distributes his presents
And brings great joy.

Father Christmas distributes presents to children

The Christmas Lunch
(English Folklore)

Yummy! Don't you want to eat it too?

On the first day
Of Christmas week,
Father brought home
A huge turkey.

Two partridges
On the second day
To the house
Made their way.

On the third day
Of Christmas week,
He brought home
Smoked salmon three.

Four pounds of butter,
On day four,
On the fifth day
Five bags of flour.

The Christmas Lunch

On the sixth day Of Christmas week,
Came sacks of walnuts
Numbering six.

Baskets of mandarin
Numbering seven,
On the seventh day,
To Mother were given.

On Christmas morning
Mother dear,
Set to work
With the ingredients here.

With her love and her skill,
The table she laid,
And a mouth-watering
Christmas lunch she made.

Using little twigs of holly
To decorate
She set the table
With her best plates.

They called then
Family and Friends,
And proceeded to enjoy
Their Christmas lunch.

The Christmas lunch